LOVE LETTERS
TO
MY SCARS

LOVE LETTERS
TO
MY SCARS

The Cost of Silence —
Paid in Pieces

Michelle Rae

Michelle Rae Publishing House

Publisher: Michelle Rae Publishing House
Author: Michelle Rae
Printed in the United States of America

ISBN: 979-8-9944298-4-6

Dedication

For you.
For me.

For the version of us who shrank to fit
into places we never belonged—
and for the version of us done with
paying in pieces.

I hope these words help you name
what you've carried,
and remind you that healing isn't about erasing scars—
it's about acknowledging what hurt
and giving yourself permission to heal,
one honest moment at a time.

Table of Contents

Introduction

Silence is not empty. It holds the weight of everything we were never allowed to say without fear.

For many of us, silence wasn't a choice—it was a survival instinct. We learned early speaking came with consequences and naming pain didn't bring comfort. We also learned--what didn't bend would break--so we adapted.

We swallowed our words and hid our hurt feelings in places no one could reach. For a while, silence felt safe—until we understood what it was really costing us.

We learned how to function while something inside us quietly broke.

We learned what goes unspoken doesn't disappear, it settles into the body and, ultimately, reshapes the way we love, the way we trust, and the way we see ourselves.

Over time, silence teaches us what to tolerate and to accept. Silence becomes so familiar we adjust our reality to deceive ourselves with the lies we embrace. Our silence becomes a dysfunction we learned to normalize just to get through the day.

The cost of silence is paid in the pieces we give up when we negotiate the essence of who we are to keep from rocking the boat—even as the ship is sinking.

Scars are born from muting our voices—to belong, to be chosen, and to be accepted.

Identifying our scars is the first step toward healing. Naming them helps us understand the people, places, and patterns that no longer support our growth — or never did.

We must acknowledge the weight we carried simply by staying silent.

Once we understand our silence, we begin to recognize the power of our voice.

It is important to listen to what our scars have been telling us—about self-worth, love, strength, and survival.

We also begin to understand the importance of listening inward without allowing outside noise to decide who we become.

If you have ever felt the weight of what was left unsaid— you belong here.

This book is an invitation to listen to your inner voice and to heal internal scars you've quietly carried.

Healing doesn't come from pretending we were untouched, it begins the moment we admit what it took from us.

Silence has a price—and many of us paid it in pieces.

This is not just my story. It is ours.

Chapter 1 — The Wounds We Hide

There was a time when survival required silence.

If you pause long enough, you may feel it—not as a memory, but as something familiar. A feeling born from staying quiet while your inner voice begged to be heard, seen, or acknowledged.

Naming your pain felt dangerous, like opening a door you might never close again. So, you kept it shut and learned to live with it locked. You learned how to smile while something inside you bled in silence.

You learned early that silence could masquerade as safety, and you hid inside that illusion because the truth felt too sharp to hold.

You dressed up the lie to look productive, filling your days so completely that there was no space left to sit with yourself. Full calendars and endless to-do lists became the perfect distraction from the reflection you weren't ready to face.

You hid in humor—making people laugh so they wouldn't look too closely. You learned how to be light, likable, the one who keeps the room afloat, all while quietly steering attention away from anything that might crack you open.

You hid beneath a strength that was praised but never examined — the kind people admire because it asked nothing of them. A strength that keeps going, keeps functioning, keeps quiet and earns applause instead of concern.

Maybe — like me — you called it resilience but resilience without honesty becomes a cage.

For every pain you carried — the hurtful words, the broken trust, the unmet needs — you swallowed it. You trained yourself not to react, not to feel, and not to ask for more.

You learned how to stay composed even while something inside you was shattering. Why? Because admitting it hurt would mean something had to change.

Denial felt safer because naming the truth would require something of you — speaking up, setting boundaries, or walking away. Once again, you pretended you were fine.

You pretended it didn't matter.

You pretended you didn't feel it.

Why? Because beneath the pain was fear of being rejected, fear of being alone, and fear that honoring your truth would cost you the very thing you wanted most:

Love.

Not love as it should be — but love as you learned to accept it:

A love that required your silence.

A love that didn't love you back.

Denial became your shelter, and avoidance became a habit that blurred the lines and silenced your voice. Over time, you learn to abandon yourself without ever leaving the room.

Turning a blind eye or holding your tongue doesn't make pain disappear. Wounds don't vanish because you refuse to look at them. They just wait beneath the surface, building pressure, until something gives.

Even when you believe no one sees your scars, they do. Your scars, and mine, show up in your overthinking, over-giving, overexplaining and the way we brace for impact even in moments meant to feel safe.

These patterns don't appear out of nowhere. They grow from the lies we tell ourselves:

It didn't hurt that much.

I'm asking for too much.

This is just how it is.

These lies soften the pain just enough to keep us going, keep us upright and functioning, but lies don't heal — they only postpone the pain.

I have personally learned one thing for certain and two things for sure, postponed pain doesn't disappear. It simply waits for the moment you're too exhausted to keep pretending.

When hurt deepens scars form — not due to weakness but because we carried what was too heavy for too long.

Our bodies remember what our voices learned to hide — the stories our silence carried.

Many of us learned how to endure before learning to heal.

We believed staying quiet was safer than naming what hurt because we did not realize telling the truth wouldn't undo us. So we kept going. Staying silent worked—until it didn't.

If you're reading this now, you are ready to stop silencing your voice and to be honest about the scars you've been carrying in silence. You are standing at the door where healing begins.

Reflection

- Where did you first learn that silence felt safer than truth?

- What part of you have you been hiding the longest?

- What pain have you minimized because you didn't believe it "counted"?

- Where do you notice yourself showing strength instead of honoring your truth?

- If your scars could speak one sentence, what would they say?

Affirmations

- I am allowed to name what hurt me.

- I do not have to hide to feel safe.

- My healing begins with honesty.

Love Letter to the Wounds We Hide

Dear You,

I see the places you learned to hide and the truths you swallowed to get through the day.

Your body held what your voice couldn't carry, and every silence you swallowed left its mark on your heart.

Your cracks showed—not from weakness but they came from holding too much for too long with nowhere to put it.

Your silence cost you pieces, and still—you survived.

This is recognition for your scars — for the version of you who made it through without knowing how to heal and who learned to stay quiet because it felt necessary.

You didn't know that facing pain wouldn't break you or that naming it would loosen its grip.

You were protecting yourself the only way you knew how.

You don't need to be brave, just honest about what hurt you.

This type of honesty isn't disloyalty to who you were; it's loyalty to who you're becoming.

Honesty is the first step back to yourself.

With love,
You

Chapter 2 — The History of Our Scars

Pain is a storyteller.

It doesn't shout or announce itself. It whispers—over time, over years—until its voice feels indistinguishable from your own.

If you listen closely, you can hear it shaping how you see yourself, how you interpret love, and how you decide what you deserve.

Our pain becomes our scars, and every scar carries a story. If you sit with yourself long enough — quiet enough — you'll hear them speak back to you in reflections and lingering afterthoughts.

Not all scars are harmful, and not all of them tell the truth.

Some convince you that you were too much — or never enough. Some teach you love had limits and safety depended on staying small, agreeable, useful.

You didn't question those stories. You lived them. You carried them as truth because they were familiar, and familiarity has a way of disguising itself as truth.

Beliefs formed early—especially in moments of pain— root deeply within you and become the lens through which everything else is filtered, normalized, and rarely questioned.

It is not until later you realize what once helped you survive may not be what helps you to heal.

My scars taught me to anticipate abandonment — to read rooms like warnings and feel the slightest shifts in tone long before they became words.

In some instances, my scars taught me to prepare for loss before it happened—self-sabotage.

I negotiated my value each time I silenced my voice.

Somewhere along the way, my self-worth became tangled with endurance—measured by how much I could tolerate and how far I could bend without breaking.

I edited myself—softened my needs, filtered my feelings, trimmed the edges of who I was—just to fit into spaces I wanted to belong.

I convinced myself that leaving parts of me behind was the opportunity cost of connection.

My scars taught me that belonging required negotiation, and the first thing on the table was always me—and in the moment, it made sense.

I don't believe I am alone. Have you ever silenced your voice—hoping things would change while slowly losing pieces of yourself along the way.

It's important to understand that scars don't always speak in logic; they speak from memory. Scars remember the ache, the abandonment, the silence — and what it took to survive difficult moments.

When my scars guided me toward shrinking, smoothing, or disappearing, it wasn't malice — it was muscle memory. The wounded parts of me chose the route of least resistance, believing that safety lived in self-abandonment.

I was never meant to earn connection by erasing myself or silencing my voice. Neither were you.

Scars are messengers shaped by moments you and I didn't always choose. They formed in response to pain—armor built in the exact moments we needed refuge—protection when we didn't have words, power, or clarity to choose differently.

This isn't about silencing those stories.

It's about learning to hear the difference between the voice of fear and the voice of truth.

It's about recognizing that our scars speak from moments of threat—from what we learned when love felt uncertain, or when safety felt fragile—not from who we truly are.

You are not your coping mechanism.

You are not the beliefs you formed to survive.

You are not the story your pain told you to keep you in bondage.

When you begin to see that— and start to question the narratives you once accepted—something shifts.

You gain choice, clarity and the ability to honor your scars without letting them decide your future.

Reflection

- What belief about yourself have you accepted—without ever choosing it?

- When do you notice yourself becoming smaller, quieter, or more agreeable to feel safe?

- Where are you over giving, overexplaining, or overperforming to earn love or avoid loss?

- What is the fear underneath that pattern—and what is it trying to protect you from?

- What truth do you already know, but have been afraid to say out loud?

Affirmations

- I can honor what protected me without living there forever.

- I am allowed to outgrow the stories that kept me safe.

- I choose truth over familiar pain.

Love Letter to the History of Our Scars

Dear You,

Every scar has a history.

Not just of what happened—but of what you learned because of it.

These stories didn't arrive loudly; they settled in quietly.

They shaped how you saw yourself, what you accepted, and what you believed you had to earn.

You didn't question them.

You lived them, and they felt like the truth because they were familiar and formed in places where you were still learning how to survive difficult moments.

Some beliefs took root before you had words or a choice. They held fast not because they were right, but because they became your coping mechanism of choice.

This isn't about undoing the past. It's about seeing it clearly and understanding what once protected you doesn't have to define you forever.

You are allowed to look at the history of your scars without letting it decide your future.

You are allowed to honor what carried you through and choose differently now.

This isn't rejection of who you were but acceptance.

With love,
You

Chapter 3 — The Scars We Embraced

There are moments that divide life into before and after.

You know them—not always because they were loud or dramatic, but because something inside of you shifted and never quite returned to the way it was.

The kind of moments that rearrange your inner landscape without asking permission.

Losses that lingered long after they were supposed to be over.

Words spoken casually—or cruelly without thought— that lodge themselves so deeply within you they echoed for years.

Your scars were born in moments like these.

Not all of them announced themselves as trauma. Some arrived quietly, disguised as disappointment, neglect, misunderstanding, or love that asked too much of you.

You survived these moments and convinced yourself it wasn't that bad because survival has a way of minimizing pain—especially when acknowledging it feels like it might undo you.

Sometimes hurt comes from a place of absence—from the spaces where care should have been but wasn't; sometimes hurt lives in the moments when you learned that needing too much, or asking for reassurance, might cost you connection—so you stayed silent.

Some scars formed in the seasons you put yourself second and kept giving long after you were empty.

Each moment left its mark—not always visible but powerful enough to shift your inner landscape.

These marks break you from the inside out, not all at once, but slowly and quietly.

You break in ways that are easy to overlook by people who only had the capacity to interpret your silence as strength.

You kept showing up — the reliable one, the strong one, the one who could "handle it" — so your hurt went unnoticed.

You learned to minimize what happened to you, and that minimization slowly distorted your judgment.

You learned to numb your pain and avoid the truth of your reality — but reality doesn't require your acknowledgment to exist.

Your experiences taught you to anticipate loss, brace for disappointment, and hold yourself together without skipping a beat.

What you went through mattered, even if no one else saw it or no one else named it. Even when people praised you for holding it together, oblivious to your pain, it still mattered.

What shaped you doesn't disappear just because it was handled quietly. It lives on in the ways you learned to adapt.

Once you can separate what happened from who you are—and give yourself grace—when you honor your scars with compassion, pain loses its stronghold.

You start to see what broke you open also made space for something new: embracing your scars instead of hiding them.

You finally allow yourself to say, *this broke something open in me,* and you begin to separate who you had to be in survival mode from who you are becoming.

You can then ask yourself, *What do I need now?*

Reflection

- What moment still echoes in you—even if you rarely speak of it?

- What did you need then that you did not receive?

- In what ways did you minimize your pain to make it easier to survive?

- Where are you still carrying the impact of that moment in your life today?

- What would it mean to say—out loud or on paper—"This mattered."

Affirmations

- What happened to me mattered.

- I can honor my past without living inside it.

- I deserve healing that is honest and whole.

Love Letter to the Scars We Embraced

Dear You,

Some moments change everything, not with noise, but with an internal shift you can't undo.

You didn't always recognize these moments as wounds. Most arrived quietly—as disappointment you learned to live with, as being overlooked, as love that asked more of you than it gave back.

You survived them, so you told yourself they didn't matter. If you could carry them, they must not have been that heavy.

Pain dulls itself when naming it feels overwhelming—but naming it is how you move through the scars that came from trusting or leaning in without knowing you should have walked away.

You had to choose your broken pieces by embracing what they represented. Your embrace was an acknowledgment of what was lost and what you gave away.

You gathered what you survived and let it belong to you again — not to return to the pain, but to become whole.

It is time for you to embrace you.

With love,
You

Chapter 4 — The Silence Within

Silence became your second language--not all at once and not by choice, but gradually you learned how to disappear in plain sight.

You learned how to function while feeling hollow inside.

You learned to keep showing up even as something inside you went quiet.

I know I did.

I learned numbness felt safer than sorrow and emotional detachment felt cleaner than emotions.

If I didn't feel too deeply I thought I would control the depth of my pain.

I learned to dim my own light just enough to make it through the day without showcasing my pain.

I learned to live inside of silence.

I coped by staying busy and agreeable.

I coped by staying emotionally unavailable to my own feelings.

I told myself I was strong because I didn't cry aloud, I kept moving, and I didn't ask for help.

I wore self-sufficiency like armor and mistook endurance for healing.

I silently betrayed myself to fit into someone's profile of who I should be, or needed to be, as a condition of acceptance.

Have you ever smiled through conversations while something inside you withdrew further inward.

Over time, the line between who you were and who you were becoming softened until it disappeared.

You became good at being who everyone else needed you to be and stopped being who you needed to be for yourself. You knew you could return to "you" later, but often later was met with silence.

Silence carried you when expression felt costly and shielded you when honesty came with consequences.

Silence helped you endure when healing wasn't yet possible.

You were never meant to live in that space where safety came from swallowing your own voice.

You were never meant to build a life that required you to disappear in order to be accepted.

There comes a moment, quiet at first, when hiding begins to hurt more than honesty.

When pretending becomes heavier than truth and when shrinking starts to feel like suffocation.

You grow tired of going along just to get along.

That moment isn't selfish—it's an awakening when you finally look past the reflection shaped by pain and reach inward—toward the part of you that already knew something had to change.

This is the moment you choose yourself, not above anyone else but alongside your own needs.

It is at this moment, your scars start to look different.

The ones you hid in silence were never signs of weakness.

They were quiet proof that you carried more than you should have held.

You endured what you were never meant to hold alone.

Your scars don't need to be hidden now.

They don't need explanation or permission to exist.

Your scars tell a story of strength, of worth, and of someone who made it through and no longer agrees to disappear just to belong.

You are here.

You have arrived.

You are here to stay.

Reflection

- Where have you been disappearing in plain sight?

- What emotions have you been avoiding because they feel too heavy to hold?

- What has your silence been protecting you from admitting—about a person, a pattern, or yourself?

- Where are you worn out from acting strong instead of being honest about what's real for you?

- What truth are you ready to stop carrying alone?

Affirmations

- I do not have to disappear to belong.

- My voice is allowed to take up space.

- I am ready to live honestly, not quietly.

Love Letter to the Silence Within

Dear You,

Silence didn't arrive all at once, it learned you slowly.

You learned how to move through the world while keeping parts of yourself out of reach.

You kept going even through the pain, not because it was easy but because stopping wasn't an option yet.

You learned how to move through the world without letting it touch you too deeply.

How to stay present without being exposed.

How to protect what was tender by keeping it just out of reach.

You told yourself this was strength. Needing less meant being safer and carrying it alone was proof you could handle whatever came.

For a time, it worked. It got you through.

What you called strength was really a pause—a way of holding yourself together until you were ready to feel again and find your voice.

You didn't reclaim it all at once. You let it return slowly—in pauses, in truth spoken under your breath, in moments where you chose to speak even when it felt unfamiliar because it was necessary.

You don't have to be silent anymore. Your voice matters, your scars matter—you matter.

With love,
You

Chapter 5 — Our Alter Egos

There are many versions of you living inside your scars, and none of them appeared overnight.

They formed slowly—layer by layer, moment by moment—long before you had the words to name what you were seeing.

By the time you grew older, those early impressions had already begun shaping your behaviors, your patterns, your relationships, but the truth reaches even further beneath the surface.

Many scars do not begin with obvious harm. They form in inconsistency — in environments where:

Love was genuine, yet unpredictable

Care existed, but conditions shifted

Emotional safety was not threatened, but was unreliable

You learned early that connection could change without warning—that affection could feel warm one moment and far away the next.

You didn't imagine this.

You noticed it because the younger you were paying attention--listening for tones, reading moods and tracking shifts.

You sensed when it was better to speak and when silence felt safer.

You adapted—not out of fear, but out of a sincere attempt to understand how love worked.

Although it was a flawed and inconsistent model, it was the one you anchored your decisions on well into adulthood.

That version of you still lives within you.

The one who became observant, accommodating, thoughtful.

The one who learned to read a room, soften needs, and meet others where they were—sometimes at your own expense.

That younger you did not fail you.

They were learning the rules as they were given, not out of weakness, but out of a genuine desire to be accepted.

Then came the teenager.

The version of you who learned to harden.

The one who felt the pressure to belong, to be chosen, to not fall behind.

You bent yourself around peer expectations and unspoken rules. All of it carved its way into you, and you absorbed it— because long before then, you had already learned how to adjust to the temperature of any room.

You learned to go along to get along.

You learned to quiet your instincts in exchange for approval.

You learned to be outwardly strong even when you felt weak inside.

That teenager didn't betray you either. They were surviving a world that often punishes vulnerability.

Then came the adult.

The one who kept choosing everyone else.

The one who found themselves caught in repeating patterns.

The one who returned to dysfunction not because it felt good, but because it felt familiar.

You didn't choose these patterns with awareness; you inherited them.

You were shaped by the scars of your past.

Each version held the weight of what came before, believing endurance was love, tolerance was strength, and staying was proof of worth.

For a long time, you may have judged these versions of yourself.

You may have wondered why you didn't leave sooner, speak up louder, know better but judgment is easy in hindsight— and harsh when directed at the parts of you that simply did not know better.

The truth is: these versions were familiar and familiarity can be very persuasive.

You judged yourself while repeating the same cycles— because change required facing pain you weren't yet ready to touch.

Judgment deepens wounds while compassion begins to heal them, but healing doesn't start with blaming your past alter egos.

It begins with understanding the "why" of your choices and recognize every version of you was shaped by some experiences you never asked for.

You have to acknowledge the child who survived uncertainty in relationships, the teenager who carried pressure of where to fit in, and the adult who kept searching for peace unaware of the role they played in the chaos

Self-forgiveness is the bridge forward.

Forgiveness for the hurt child who absorbed pain they didn't know how to name.

Forgiveness for the hardened teenager who wanted acceptance.

Forgiveness for the adult who made choices shaped by old wounds instead of present truth.

You cannot heal what you refuse to forgive.

Self-forgiveness doesn't erase accountability— it creates room for transformation and opens the door for change.

Self-forgiveness allows you to stop repeating what shaped you and begin choosing what heals you.

To the alter egos who endured, to the ones who stayed, and to the ones who didn't know how to heal but refused to give up—honor them. They carried you this far.

Now you have the chance to carry them forward with intention, with clarity, with compassion.

Reflection

- Which version of you do you judge the most: the child, the teenager, or the adult?

- What did that version of you need that they didn't receive?

- What survival habit are you ready to stop calling a personality trait?

- Where have you been loyal to familiarity—even when it costs you peace?

- What would self-forgiveness look like in one small act this week?

Affirmations

- Every version of me was trying to protect me.

- I can offer compassion to the parts of me that endured.

- I am allowed to carry myself differently now.

Love Letter to Our Alter Egos

Dear You,

I see the care with which you learned to move through the world.

I watched how responsibility settled into who you had to become—long before you ever had a chance to understand what you needed.

The alter egos you created were not random.

Each one carried something useful—discernment, steadiness, endurance, perception.

None of it was accidental.

There was a time when awareness meant staying alert, when presence required readiness, when composure became the most reliable ground you had.

You learned those traits because you needed them and they kept you oriented, steady, and moving forward when nothing else felt certain.

They do not disappear simply because your life has changed and the terms are different.

They remain part of you—no longer in charge, but still valuable.

You are allowed to choose spaces that don't require explanation.

You are allowed to pause without consequence.

You are allowed to choose you — unapologetically.

Those earlier alter egos did their work, and you don't need to dismiss them to move on.

You only need to let them rest.

This is not a farewell to who you were or to the alter egos you created. It is an acknowledgment.

Thank you to every version of you that learned, adapted, held, and carried what was required at the time.

With love,
You

Chapter 6 — The Truth We Accepted

Healing began the moment you stopped running.

There was no single breakthrough or perfect moment of clarity.

Healing began quietly— when you finally paused long enough to notice what you had been avoiding, when stillness revealed what silence had kept tucked away.

Healing begins when you stop outrunning your own emotions and allow yourself to stand still in the presence of truth, even though it's uncomfortable.

For a long time, "feeling" felt uncomfortable. So, you learned to intellectualize pain instead of experiencing it.

You analyzed it, minimized it, and rationalized it.

You tried to fix it—because fixing felt productive, and productivity always felt safer than vulnerability, but healing does not begin with fixing. It begins with feeling.

The truth is healing begins when you let grief be grief instead of a problem to solve.

It begins when you stop asking, *How do I get past this?* and start asking, *What is this asking of me?*

Sometimes truth doesn't arrive gently.

It asks you to sit with the hurt buried beneath your busyness and to acknowledge the denial, avoidance, or distance you learned to create just to keep going.

Sometimes truth requires you to face the disappointment you kept reframing as acceptance.

It asks you to admit what you lost—or what you never received.

Sometimes truth asks you to grieve not only what happened, but what never did.

This kind of mourning is heavy because it demands honesty.

It requires admission, and admission can be a painful reckoning.

The truth will ask you to see where needs were not met, where healing never arrived, and where younger versions of you were required to grow up too soon—or quietly disappear.

The truth stripped away the stories you used to survive:

It wasn't that bad.

Others had it worse.

I should be over this by now.

Those stories helped you stay functional—but they also kept you broken.

When you finally allowed yourself to feel, your body answered first.

Your breath eased, your shoulders released and the tension you carried without noticing began to loosen.

Feeling did not undo you the way you once feared. It opened something—it freed you.

There is relief in honesty that avoidance can never offer.

Relief in naming what hurt without immediately justifying it, explaining it away, or reshaping it into something more acceptable.

Turning toward the hurt is one of the bravest things you can ever do. Allowing yourself to feel it — instead of denying it — is what begins to loosen its grip.

We don't stay stuck because healing is impossible; we stay stuck because feeling *feels* unbearable and we soften the truth until it's unrecognizable.

We call abandonment "miscommunication," neglect "independence," and emotional starvation "strength."

We deny what is obvious, even when it stands right in front of us.

Denial numbs pain for a moment, but we cannot heal from we refuse to name.

There is relief in allowing pain to exist - to let it be felt, honored, and finally released.

Healing requires honesty and the ability to remain present when discomfort arises, without rushing to outrun it or explain it away.

Patience and gentleness also matter, not because the truth is fragile, but because you are meeting it with care.

Accepting the truth is not weakness. It is courage—quiet, deliberate, and earned.

The truth did not arrive to punish you; it came to release you and reconnect you with yourself.

You did not break when you finally let yourself feel and accept the truth.

You became whole and healing finally had somewhere to begin.

Reflection

- What feeling have you been avoiding the most: grief, anger, disappointment, shame, or longing?

- What "story" have you been using to minimize your pain?

- Where do you try to fix what you actually need to feel?

- What truth would your healing require you to stop editing?

- What would it look like to sit with your feelings without abandoning yourself?

Affirmations

- I am allowed to feel what I feel without explaining it away.

- The truth is not here to punish me—it is here to free me.

- I can be honest with myself and still be safe.

Love Letter to the Truth We Accepted

Dear You,

Healing starts the moment you allow yourself to listen to what is asking for your attention.

For a long time, *feeling* felt unsafe.

You learned to stay elsewhere — in thought, in explanation, in making sense of what hurt so it could be carried without spilling over.

That wasn't avoidance; it was care, shaped by necessity.

Truth doesn't ask to be managed, reframed, or softened, it asks to be met with boldness.

When you finally allowed that—when you stopped bargaining and let what was present remain—nothing fell apart.

You didn't disappear beneath it.

You stayed.

> You breathed.

> > You learned that feeling could move through you without undoing you.

This letter honors that moment.

The moment you stopped resisting and allowed the truth to exist without dressing it up or down.

With love,
You

Chapter 7 — The Healing We Deserve

Healing was not loud.

It did not arrive with certainty or clarity.

It did not announce itself with breakthroughs or grand declarations.

Healing came quietly—so quietly you almost missed it.

It arrived in small, ordinary moments that didn't look like transformation at all.

It showed up in choices.

In the boundaries you set and immediately questioned.

In the pauses before saying no when you were used to saying yes.

Healing showed up in the rest that felt undeserved, unearned, even uncomfortable.

It also showed in the self-forgiveness that unfolded slowly and imperfectly, not as a single release, but as something you had to return to again and again.

For a long time, you believed healing had to hurt to be real and peace was earned through suffering.

You thought softness signaled weakness.

Healing asked you to unlearn all of this and remain gentle without becoming passive.

You had to learn openness without abandoning yourself and softness without losing strength.

Strength has many faces and it doesn't look the same to everyone.

Sometimes strength is refusing to overcompensate for someone else's behavior.

Sometimes strength is breaking patterns that keep asking too much of you.

Sometimes strength is walking away from what is costing you too much, not just financially, but emotionally and mentally.

Strength is making a conscious decision to choose yourself, even when it feels uncomfortable.

At some point, you bought into the belief that you were not worthy of care — or worse, that you deserved the treatment you received.

You believed if you were hurt, it must have been your fault, or you had done something to earn the pain.

You blamed yourself.

You told yourself you were too sensitive, too much, or not enough.

You stayed in places that made you smaller and rationalized behavior that cut deeper than you admitted.

You measured your pain against someone else's and convinced yourself that *your* pain didn't count.

Comparison became another form of avoidance. As long as your attention stayed outward—measuring, minimizing, rationalizing—you didn't have to turn toward what was calling for you on the inside.

You didn't have to face the unfamiliar work of caring for yourself in ways no one ever modeled for you.

Healing required a shift in direction and a willingness to meet yourself where you had been waiting to be chosen.

You had to move away from fixing others, away from proving your worth, away from justifying pain— and turn toward honoring yourself.

You began rebuilding trust in small, almost unnoticeable ways — by honoring the signals you once overrode with flawed logic.

You allowed your intuition to speak without immediately silencing your internal voice.

Trust returned slowly— in the moments you chose yourself, in the boundaries you held, and in truth you stopped negotiating.

Self-trust grew in the moments you chose not to dismiss what your heart knew.

It continued to grow in moments when you listened to your body speak without dismissal when something felt off.

It grew each time you stopped bartering and trading the essence of you — each time you chose yourself instead of abandoning what you knew to be true— with every one of those choices, you stepped closer to yourself.

Every time you let your truth stand without softening for someone else's comfort and for every moment you stood up for yourself — you found your way back home to "you."

You learned that healing doesn't ask for perfection — only your presence.

It asks for compassion where judgment once lived, and patience for the parts of you still learning what emotional safety feels like.

Healing asks for the courage to believe you are worthy of care — and to accept that you deserve it.

Healing didn't come to correct you or punish you.

It came to open a future where you no longer have to shrink to stay connected and where belonging doesn't require disappearing.

It's a future where you are free to take up space without apology.

Reflection

- Where do you still believe you have to earn rest, peace, or love?

- What boundary have you set recently that you keep questioning?

- Where do you override your intuition to keep the peace or avoid conflict?

- What would it look like to treat your needs as valid without defending them?

- What is one way you can choose yourself this week— without apology?

Affirmations

- I do not have to earn what I deserve.

- My needs are valid, even when they are inconvenient to others.

- I can choose myself and still be a good person.

Love Letter to the Healing We Deserve

Dear You,

Healing didn't arrive with answers.

It showed up quietly in the moments you slowed down, in choices you questioned, and in the pauses where you listened instead of overriding yourself just to keep things smooth.

It showed up each time you honored a boundary instead of betraying it and each time you rested without apology.

Healing arrived each time you chose care where criticism once lived, and each time you allowed healing to be messy and still true.

For a long time, you believed healing had to hurt and peace required sacrifice.

You thought rest was something earned only after you had given everything away and then, slowly, you began to unlearn that falsity.

You learned how to be gentle without shrinking yourself, and how to stay open without betraying your own needs.

Strength began to look like choosing yourself, even when that choice meant letting relationships end.

This is the healing meant for you.

The kind that doesn't ask you to hurt first.

The kind that lets you be imperfect — without punishment.

With love,
You

Chapter 8 — The Strength We Found

There comes a moment when you realize your scars no longer ache in the same way. They don't require the attention it once demanded.

Your scars did not weaken you; they refined you.

What once felt like damage slowly revealed itself as depth.

What once felt like anxiety became discernment.

You did not come out of pain untouched; you came out awake.

You became more aware and grounded in yourself than you had ever been before.

The strength you carry now did not come from pretending you were never hurt. It came from staying present with *what hurt*, and refusing to let it turn you bitter.

Your scars taught you empathy—the kind that listens instead of fixes.

They taught you resilience—not the kind that endures endlessly, but the kind that knows when to stop and walk away.

Your scars taught you discernment—the ability to tell the difference between familiarity and safety, intensity and intimacy, and actions and words.

For a long time, you believed strength meant pushing through, ignoring signals, and minimizing your needs.

You mistook self-abandonment for discipline, as if disappearing or shrinking yourself was a skill you were meant to master.

Strength is facing the truth without breaking beneath it.

41

Strength is refusing to surrender pieces of yourself just to earn a seat at a table where your presence is not respected.

Strength is not the absence of pain, but the ability to face it without abandoning yourself in the process.

You are strong because you refused to let hurt decide who you would become.

You are strong because you survived people, places, and patterns that tried to break you.

You are strong because you noticed when something no longer served you, and you adjusted your behavior instead of pretending you didn't see the difference.

You stopped playing by the rules that once kept you small.

Breaking patterns is not easy work. It asks you to choose the unfamiliar over what once felt comfortable, and to choose yourself in moments where choosing others had become a reflex.

The strength you found in the places that hurt is quiet, grounded, and undeniable. It does not announce itself or apologize for being present.

Your strength shows in the way you move through the world now—with clearer boundaries, deeper compassion, and a self-trust that no longer asks for permission.

This is the strength you carried all along. It was never absent. You buried it beneath the voice you learned to silence out of fear of losing something, without realizing you were losing yourself each time you shrank to fit into rooms you didn't belong.

You don't have to do that anymore.

Reflection

- Where have you confused intensity with intimacy in the past?

- What pattern have you broken that you're still learning to trust?

- Where are you practicing strength by stopping instead of pushing through?

- What boundary are you proud of—even if it still feels uncomfortable?

- What does your strength look like now that you're no longer in survival mode?

Affirmations

- I can be strong without becoming hard.

- I trust myself to recognize what is safe.

- I am allowed to grow beyond what once hurt me.

Love Letter to the Strength We Found

Dear You,

There came a moment when your scars stopped asking for attention because they no longer carried the same weight.

Your scars softened enough to hold clarity and perspective without compromising the truth.

Your scars made you strong—not by what they took from you, but by what they taught you to notice.

What once felt like damage settled into understanding.

You didn't come through unaffected; you came through aware and grounded in what you feel.

You are no longer willing to abandon yourself for acceptance.

The strength you carry now didn't come from pretending you were never hurt, it came from acknowledging your pain.

You learned how to protect yourself without disappearing and how to remain open without losing your edge.

You are strong because you survived.

You are strong because your scars have taught you how to live without leaving yourself behind.

With love,
You

Chapter 9 — Love Letter to Becoming

Dear You,

There came a moment when you gathered yourself— not all at once, nor neatly, but honestly.

You recognized your growth and for a long time, it felt like a betrayal to name anything gained — as if acknowledging growth required you to excuse what was lost.

Or recognizing strength was a silent admission the pain was acceptable, but it never was acceptable.

What happened mattered.

It hurt and it did not get the final word.

Thank you for enduring what you were never given support for and through.

Thank you for moving through seasons where silence felt safer than truth—even when that silence cost you pieces of yourself.

Thank you for remaining present in spaces where being seen came at a cost.

Silence protected you and it also asked too much of you.

It taught you to discount your worth, to swallow your voice, and to scatter parts of yourself in exchange for acceptance— piece by piece, memory by memory, truth by truth.

Thank you for the versions of you that hid, for the versions that stayed alert and for the versions of you created to stay intact when your footing felt unsteady.

Thank you for the alter egos who learned to disappear in plain sight because visibility required too much.

You were not weak.

You were perceptive.

Thank you for listening to the versions of you who would not stay quiet anymore.

Thank you for stopping long enough to feel what you once had to outrun.

Thank you for accepting what was real without letting it imprison you.

Your scars did not ask to be fixed, they asked to be heard.

They did not ask for pity, they demanded change.

Your scars showed you where your boundaries belong.

Your scars taught you what to no longer tolerate.

Your scars showed you what mattered and what never truly did.

They revealed the cost of abandoning yourself, and the benefits that came from choosing differently.

Through your scars, you learned your limits, your values, and your worth.

You learned not everything deserves your energy or access to your heart.

You learned love without respect is not love at all.

Your scars no longer feel like evidence of failure; they feel like proof of becoming.

Becoming arrived as recognition—the moment you stopped breaking yourself to fit where you never belong.

Becoming was realizing your value even when others attempted to diminish your worth.

Your scars remind you of how far you've come—not in distance, but in depth.

They remind you of how much you've learned and how deeply you've grown by honoring your needs.

I love every version of you.

The child who did the best they could, the younger self who learned to adjust, and the adult who made costly choices in pursuit of happiness.

I love every scar—not for what it took, but for what it revealed, for the truth it required, and for the pieces it led you back to.

You are whole, not because you didn't break, but because you gathered yourself anyway.

You are whole because your pieces have always belonged to you.

This is not the end of the story.

This is the beginning of belonging to yourself—with boundaries, with softness, with self-trust, and with a heart that no longer abandons itself just to be chosen.

This is where you move at the pace your healing asks for—not rushed, not forced, not performative.

This is where truth is anchored in healing—without regret, without shame, and without leaving yourself behind.

With love,
You

Epilogue — When Silence Speaks

You didn't arrive here by accident.

If you're holding this book, it's likely because something in you recognized yourself in these pages—the pauses, the quiet endurance, the parts of you that learned how to survive without ever being asked what they needed.

This book was never meant to fix you.

It was meant to help you gather your pieces.

Silence once helped you adapt and endure, but silence was never meant to be your home. It was shelter, a season, and a way through.

There comes a point when you realize what once protected you can no longer lead you, not because the protection wasn't necessary, but because you have grown beyond that need.

You are ready for more.

Your scars are evidence of what you carried, what you learned and evidence that something in you kept choosing to move forward—even when you couldn't yet see where forward would take you.

May you leave this book a little more compassionate toward your past and hopeful for your future and always remember:

You are allowed to choose yourself without explanation.

You are allowed to rest without guilt.

You are allowed to release what was never yours to carry.

About the Author

Michelle Rae writes from the quiet places where truth meets tenderness. As the creator of Scarlet Love Notes and the author of *Shattered Depths* and *Pick Up Your Pieces*, she offers language for the wounds we learn to hide and the strength we forget we carry.

Her work is shaped by emotional honesty, gentle self-inquiry, and the belief that healing begins the moment we stop silencing ourselves. Through reflections that honor both the weight of what was lost and the courage it takes to reclaim what remains, Michelle invites readers to return to themselves with compassion and clarity — reminding them that every piece they thought was gone was simply waiting to be reclaimed.

Love Letters to My Scars continues her commitment to writing that doesn't rush your becoming — words that make room for truth, for softness, and for the quiet rebuilding that happens when you finally choose yourself.